JUMP START

No-Cost Online Solar Business For Anyone

Nasir Qureshi,

"Realtor Daddy"

Nasir Qureshi, Realtor®

TREC LIC. # 0792478

Texas Signature Realty

2323 S. Voss Road, Suite 315 C

Houston, Texas 77057

Direct: (281) 857-2000

www.realtordaddy.com

Copyright © 2024 by Nasir W. Qureshi

All rights reserved. No part of this book may be reproduced or transmitted in any form or by any means — graphic, electronic, or mechanical, including photocopying, recording, or any information storage or retrieval system — for sale without permission from the publisher, except for brief quotations included in a review.

This book is designed to provide general information. It is with the understanding that the publisher and author are not engaged in rendering specific legal, tax, accounting, or other professional advice or services. If legal or other expert assistance is required, seek the services of a competent professional. I do not guarantee an outcome you may or may not get by reading this book.

Published by

Nasir Qureshi Realtor®

Houston, Texas, USA

Download My Digital Business Card by Visiting

www.oneminute.today

Or Scan below

MY GIFT TO YOU

Please enter your e-mail address at www.oneminute.today to get my newsletter. Also, I can do free training for your team and/or your real estate brokerage or your company if you like. It could be online or offline, depending on my schedule and location.

TABLE CONTENTS

INTRODUCTION 8

ONE MINUTE PRESENTATION 9

IS SOLAR ENERGY BUSINESS WORTH DOING IT? 11

AMERICA IS FACING A SOLAR POWER EXPLOSION UNMATCHED IN HISTORY 15

RENEWABLES ARE ON THE RISE IN THE UNITED STATES 18

#1 BUSINESS OPPORTUNITY ON THE PLANET 20

100 COST-EFFECTIVE WAYS TO GET SOLAR ENERGY BUSIENSS LEADS FOR ANYONE 22

MILLION DOLLAR QUESTION 27

"WOULD IT BE OK TO HAVE A FIXED-LOW ELECTRICITY BILL?" 28

LEARN-AND-EARN PROGRAM 31

FACTS & LEGAL RESEACH 33

I AM A GREEN REALTOR 35

MY GREEN DESIGNATION FROM THE NATIONAL ASSOCIATION OF REALTORS 38

ABOUT THE AUTHOR 40

OTHER BOOKS BY THE AUTHOR ARE AVAILABLE ON AMAZON 41

MY GIFT FOR YOU...46

REQUEST FOR YOUR KIND REVIEW 47

INTRODUCTION

Most of the people decide to do a business or not to do a business by thinking if they can do it or not? This thought has not much to do with the business itself they are considering. Rather, it has more to do with the people themselves. Their background, personalities, abilities, skills, lack of skills, strengths, weaknesses, and good or bad past business experiences etc.

But here is the good news about doing solar energy business with us. United for Solar, LLC partnered with Apricot Solar and others. Anyone can do it. There is an old saying "when there is a will, there is a way". This old saying truly fits our unique solar energy business model.

Now the remaining question is, are you willing to do the business for your own reasons that you know better than anyone else? Meanings, it is not that important how you would do it? But what more important is do you want to do it?

To answer the question of how you can do it. I made things easier for you. In this book, I have outlined what is happening in America and in the world when it comes to solar energy and renewable energy industry. What will continue to happen? Some facts and legal research and 100 cost-effective ways to get solar energy business leads for anyone.

Let's begin!

ONE MINUTE PRESENTATION

Everyone is looking to make an extra income these days. Speaking of inflation, everything costs more these days. Everything has gone up except our salaries.

Some people drive cars as rideshare to make an extra living. Some people are delivering food. Some people rent extra space in the app. Some people do affiliate marketing online or anything else. But there is no app, side gig or affiliate marketing that pays more than this business in the most fastest growing industry in the U.S. <u>THE ONE-MINUTE PRESENTATION</u>

"People make referrals everyday but don't get paid for it. With us you will, so don't change anything.

We are a solar energy company. Helping homeowners in the U.S. since 2011 with $0 down, 25 years production guarantee, fixed low bill enabling homeowners thousands of dollars in financial benefit when they go solar.

Everyone knows homeowners with high electric bills. We use an educational approach as an option for homeowners to save money. Our top earners work from home. There is no startup cost, no monthly or yearly fee. No door knocking, cold calling, selling, recruiting or installation.

You will earn up to $7000 as our partner or $500 referral fee as our affiliate. Our solar experts will train you. Refer homeowners and we will do the rest. Refer, earn, and repeat. Thank you!"

Same one-minute presentation of our business can be viewed in an explainer video here https://linktr.ee/solarusa

You can call **720-708-1210** now and listen to the same one-minute presentation pre-recorded and leave a message. A hiring manager will contact you for an interview to help you get started.

IS SOLAR ENERGY BUSINESS WORTH DOING IT?

Google "Executive Order 14057". You will get a first hit from an executive order from The White House. An executive order from the President of The United States of America, Joe Biden.

https://www.whitehouse.gov/briefing-room/presidential-actions/2021/12/08/executive-order-on-catalyzing-clean-energy-industries-and-jobs-through-federal-sustainability/

Now, we are not having a political debate here of being republican or a democrat. But you would agree with me that a President of the United States of America has more credibility than me. So instead of believing in me. Believe in what the President is saying regardless of what political party he belongs to or not.

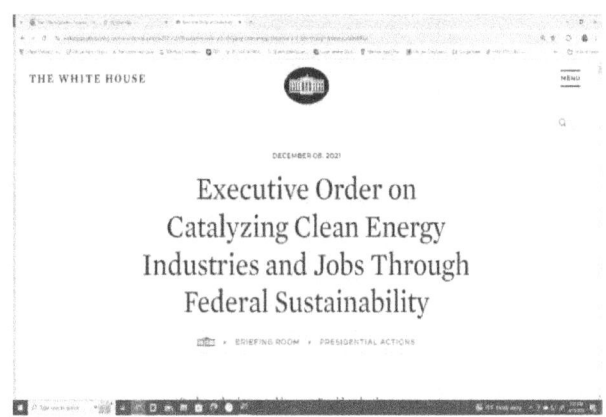

Scroll all the way down and you will see President Joe Biden's name.

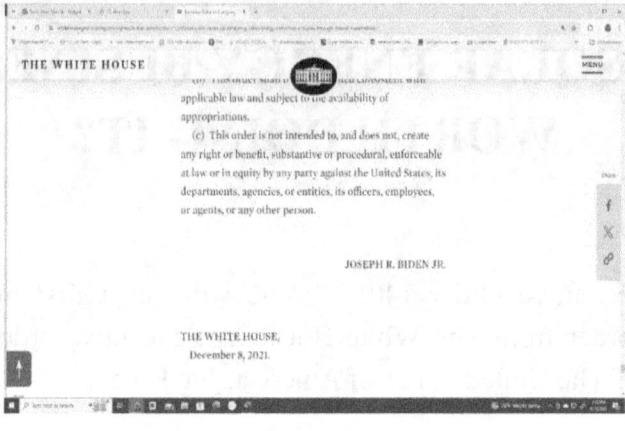

Then, scroll all the way up again. Go to paragraph 4 and read line 1-4.

Lines 1-4, give us the window into what is already happening in America and what will continue to happen in America until 2050. This is not coming from a business salesman pitch that trying to sign you up. It's coming from the President of the United States.

This means that the entire United States will go solar and/or renewable energy by 2050 whether we like it or not, whether we understand it or not. Why? Because the world is in trouble by change in the climate.

There are approximately 100 million single family homes in the United States. Only 3 million homes and rapidly growing have solar. By 2034 all homes are expected to go solar. Want to see proof?

https://www.cnet.com/home/energy-and-utilities/why-the-us-added-a-record-amount-of-solar-power-in-2023/

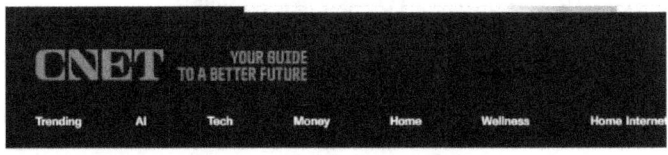

With solar payback periods potentially increasing in key states, it's uncertain whether rooftop installation will remain popular -- or if solar leases, power purchase agreements or community solar programs will grow in their stead.

A sunny forecast for solar power?

According to the SEIA and Wood Mackenzie, solar capacity is expected to be able to power 100 million homes by 2034.

"If we stay the course with our federal clean energy policies, total solar deployment will quadruple over the next 10 years," said SEIA president and CEO Abigail Ross Hopper.

AMERICA IS FACING A SOLAR POWER EXPLOSION UNMATCHED IN HISTORY

https://www.popularmechanics.com/science/green-tech/a60130391/solar-breaks-record-2023/

Popular mechanics has a great article published on March 12, 2024. The link to the article is above.

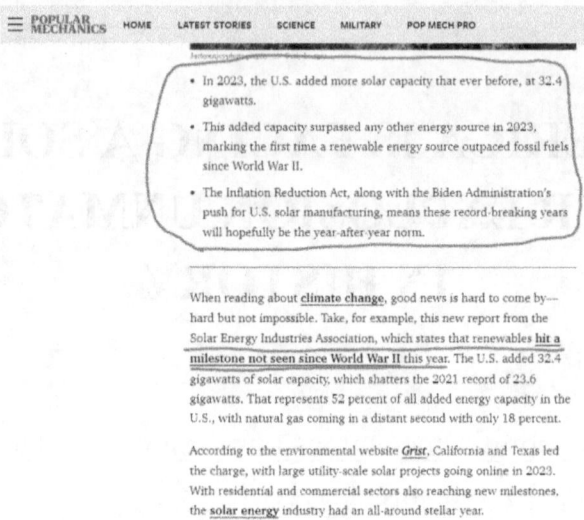

"Solar Energy Industries Association, which states that renewables hit a milestone not seen since World War II this year.

"This solar boom can be attributed to a few things – chief among them the Inflation Reduction Act (IRA), which set aside roughly $369 billion for investment in and production of clean energy, tech, as well as major incentives for installing rooftop solar."

RENEWABLES ARE ON THE RISE IN THE UNITED STATES

Today, the United States produces more than 3 times as much energy from the sun, the wind and the earth as we did just a decade ago.

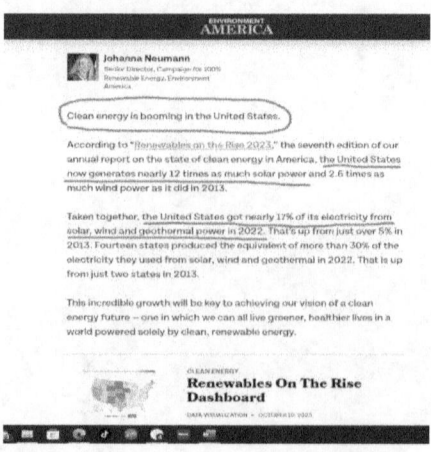

"The United States now generates nearly 12 times as much solar power and 2. 6 times as much wind power as it did in 2013."

#1 BUSINESS OPPORTUNITY ON THE PLANET

Now we know that solar and renewable energy is on the rise like nothing else in the history of America. I will not bore you with more articles and citations.

I have been in the energy industry since 2015 and I have done business from the comfort of my own home. After years of searching for the right companies, doing due diligence, legal research, and fact findings. I found and partnered with a company called "Apricot Solar" that is based in Las Vegas, Nevada.

Together with Apricot solar, my company United for Solar, LLC is building a massive team of solar advisors who can work from the comfort of their own homes and make decent money. Providing homeowners across the United States solar energy education and helping them to switch to solar.

Let's evaluate Apricot Solar business opportunity for anyone.

The #1 Business Opportunity on the Planet. Here is why:

1. ZERO financial investment and ZERO monthly cost = ZERO RISK.
2. ZERO overhead expenses like rent, utilities, payroll etc.
3. Less than 3% market penetration. Over $500 billion annual industry.
4. ZERO competition in the market. (#1 largest solar energy company. 6 years in a row on Inc. 5000 list).

5. No cold calling, door knocking-has proven warm market referral lead system.
6. 100 % virtual – make money online anywhere in the world.
7. NO NEW money out of pocket for your clients.
8. Help save clients over $100,000 as their financial benefit when they go solar with us. Further, your clients can earn up to $1000 when they give you a referral that goes solar with us.
9. The U.S. government is promoting our industry and want people to go solar. Helping people pay for their solar system with 30% tax credit.
10. You can make $10,000 + profit in your first 30 days working from home with us if you follow our system.
11. Highest commissions ($6000 - $9000/sale) & earn $1,000,000 +/ year with a small team.
12. You can hire an unlimited number of sales reps & earn $1000 - $3000 per team sale override commissions per sale.
13. Unlimited commissions, 100 % profit margin, legal business ownership & profit sharing.
14. A purpose driven business – help people get financially free & help save the planet.
15. A team of millionaire mentors who have a financial interest in our success and will teach you skills and help you believe in yourself to get financially free! (WIN – WIN).

Visit the link https://linktr.ee/solarusa and watch one minute presentation, sign up for a free affiliate link and contact me.

100 COST-EFFECTIVE WAYS TO GET SOLAR ENERGY BUSIENSS LEADS FOR ANYONE

1. Host a solar open house event. A private solar business zoom
2. Offer free home evaluations for solar energy systems
3. Create a solar energy blog and share helpful tips
4. Join a local networking group
5. Offer a free solar energy consultation
6. Partner with local businesses for cross-promotion
7. Host a solar energy-related webinar
8. Advertise on social media platforms like Facebook and Instagram
9. Email your database with relevant content and offers
10. Create a referral program for past clients
11. Volunteer at local events to meet potential customers
12. Create virtual tours of your listings
13. Collaborate with local photographers to create stunning property photos
14. Utilize SEO techniques to rank higher on search engine result pages
15. Offer first-time homebuyer seminars for solar energy
16. Use paid advertising to target specific audiences
17. Attend fundraisers and charity events in your community
18. Send handwritten notes to past clients and contacts
19. Create an online directory of local real estate resources, such as property inspectors and contractors

20. Host a giveaway on social media to increase engagement and attract leads
21. Use Google AdWords to target specific keywords related to real estate in your area
22. Develop a video marketing strategy for your listings
23. Buy leads from reputable sources. Search www.fiverr.com
24. Use door-to-door marketing in your target neighborhoods
25. Attend home and garden shows to meet potential customers
26. Offer to hold first-time homebuyer workshops with local lenders
27. Join a real estate agents referral network
28. Host an event for other real estate agents in your area
29. Offer free tips and advice on through social media
30. Sponsor local youth sports teams to gain exposure
31. Email past clients with market updates and new listings
32. Use retargeting ads to follow up with leads who visited your website
33. Attend local Chamber of Commerce events
34. Use personalized direct mail campaigns to target specific neighborhoods
35. Solar Energy Open House for Homeowners
36. Offer free seminars on solar business opportunities strategies
37. Use virtual reality technology to create immersive property tours showing solar systems
38. Create a professional website with a strong call-to-action for leads
39. Host a Q&A session on social media to answer solar energy-related questions
40. Use remarketing ads to target past website visitors
41. Create a referral program for local mortgage lenders, brokers, and realtors
42. Use LinkedIn to connect with potential customers and industry professionals
43. Offer loyalty incentives for repeat clients
44. Use influencer marketing to reach new customers

45. Host a giveaway for new homeowners, such as a gift card for furniture or home decor
46. Attend local home shows to showcase solar systems or show solar systems with A.I. together with your solar energy team leader
47. Develop a video series on solar energy tips
48. Use retargeting ads to follow up with abandoned cart leads
49. Use Facebook Live to showcase answer solar energy-related questions
50. Develop a professional, informative brochure to distribute at solar open houses
51. Use paid advertising to target customers actively searching for real estate services
52. Use Google My Business to appear in local search results
53. Use influencer marketing to reach new audiences
54. Host a charity event to generate buzz and support for your community
55. Develop a branded email marketing campaign
56. Create a strong social media presence with targeted advertisements and content
57. Use Canva with nice graphics for promotional materials for online or offline promotions
58. Utilize virtual solar energy systems to show how the home looks with solar panels
59. Use chatbots to answer solar-related questions and generate leads
60. Attend local festivals and events to meet new customers
61. Utilize Facebook ads to target customers by zip code
62. Create a referral program for contractors, landscapers, and other home service professionals
63. Offer a free solar energy consultation to homeowners
64. Use A/B testing to optimize your marketing campaigns
65. Host a VIP event for past clients and influencers
66. Use Google Analytics to track website visitor behavior and optimize your campaigns

67. Host a virtual solar workshop
68. Offer a solar energy education program
69. Use Instagram stories to showcase property with solar features and generate leads
70. Develop a strong online reputation through reviews and testimonials
71. Create a strong LinkedIn profile to connect with industry professionals and potential customers
72. Use influencer marketing to showcase your expertise and gain new customers
73. Do save the planet webinars and talk solar
74. Host a Facebook Live Q&A with industry experts
75. Create a blog post series on solar energy investing strategies
76. Use Google Ads to target long-tail keywords related to real estate
77. Create a strong incentive program for referrals
78. Use Facebook retargeting to follow-up with leads who clicked on your ads
79. Host influencer events to showcase
80. Use chatbots to generate leads through conversational marketing
81. Create a strong landing page with a clear call-to-action for leads
82. Offer a free warranty with any home sale for solar energy systems
83. Use video marketing to showcase your listings and differentiate yourself from other agents
84. Use Instagram influencers to reach new audiences
85. Host webinars on niche solar energy topics to attract customers
86. Save the planet home meetings.
87. Attend local Meetup groups related to real estate investing and homebuying
88. Host a neighborhood block party or event to meet potential customers
89. Offer a free solar energy savings analysis
90. Use A/B testing to optimize your website for lead generation

91. Offer a referral program for local real estate attorneys
92. Host a contest on social media to generate buzz and leads
93. Use Facebook groups to connect with potential customers and industry professionals
94. Host a virtual housewarming party for past clients
95. Offer a free home security consultation with any home purchase or solar system
96. Invite a solar energy expert and do an offline or online meeting
97. Attend local fairs and events to showcase your business
98. Go live on social media and showcase your research on solar energy or industry to educate crowds
99. Use chatbots to generate leads through conversational marketing
100. Host a customer appreciation event for past clients and influencers.

Let's Google, "salary of apricot solar advisor in Texas."

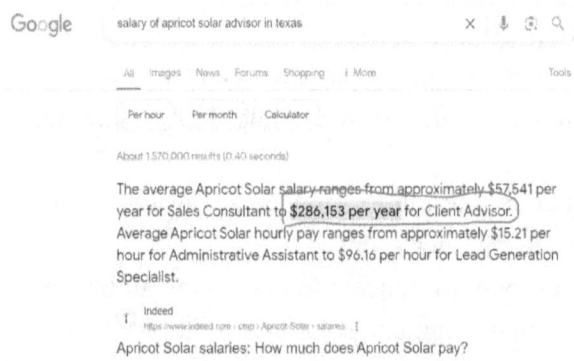

Disclaimer:

"There are no guarantees for earnings in Apricot Solar and/or with United for Solar, LLC. The success or failure of each solar advisor, like any other sales company or profession, depends upon each solar advisor's skills and worth ethic."

MILLION DOLLAR QUESTION

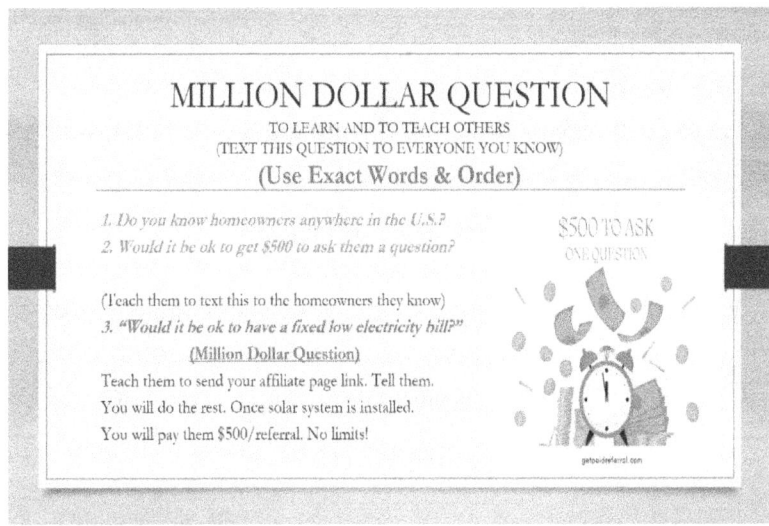

To jump start and for quicker results. Learn and memorize this question and use it anywhere and everywhere you can.

"WOULD IT BE OK TO HAVE A FIXED-LOW ELECTRICITY BILL?"

Please use exact words and do not change anything. Then, wait and see the magic.

People will reply. "YES," "SURE," OR "HOW"

When people ask yes, or how. Then, you show them a two-minute video in-person or reply to them via text from your solar affiliate page video. Titled under the page "Learn About Solar." See here.

https://solar.page/nasir-qureshi/learn

People will be able to watch a very solid and informative 2-minute video. Upload their electric bill. Then, you and I both will get an email about the lead that is being submitted. Together we will do the rest. An affiliate or referrer will get a $500 referral fee after the solar system is installed in connection with the lead.

There is no limit how many times and where you can do this. Online, offline, in person, via text or via email.

STEP 1: Create Your Free Affiliate Page Here

https://solar.page/nasir-qureshi/affiliate or www.getpaidreferral.com

You will get an email and follow instructions in your email. Visit your free affiliate page and save it or bookmark it.

STEP 2: Ask The Million Dollar Question

STEP 3: Send People to Your Affiliate Page "Learn About Solar" to get leads and electric bills. Once solar system is installed. Get paid.

We will do the rest. I will call you or you call me as well that we got a lead. I will work with you on the lead. I will do everything. Once the solar system is installed. You will get $500 for a referral or the person who has referred you this lead.

Ideas of how you can ask the "Million Dollar Question."

To the homeowners you know

You: Would it be ok to have a fixed-low electricity bill?

They: How?

You: If I send you a link to a 2-minute video, when can you watch it?

They: Right now.

You: Send them the link to your affiliate page "Learn About Solar" page. Follow up after 5 minutes.

If they ask any questions. Say, great question. An expert will answer all your questions.

To anyone you know in person or via text

I am just curious; would it be ok to have a fixed-low electricity bill?

To anyone who may know a homeowner

You: Ask them, "would it be ok to have $500 for a question?"

They: Yes, or sure.

You: Do you know any homeowners?

They: Yes.

You: Can you ask them a question that can get you $500?

They: Yes.

You: Ask them, "would it be ok to have a fixed-low electricity bill?" (they can text that to the homeowners they know).

Their homeowners will say: Yes, sure, or how?

You: Then, send them your new affiliate link of "Learn About Solar" page to watch a 2-minute video and upload their electric bill. You and I will get the lead. We will help and do the rest. We will pay $500 for a referral for your friend or anyone who asked the Million Dollar Question to the homeowner. Simple and no limits!

This way now you are leveraging other people who may know a homeowner not only the one you may know or not know.

There are approximately 100 million single family homes in the U.S. One does not have to be a homeowner to know a homeowner. So, let us be creative here.

LEARN-AND-EARN PROGRAM

The purpose of this book it to introduce you to the idea of having an online solar energy business in America. To highlight the current and future of solar energy business in America.

Further introduce you how to jump start your online solar energy business so you can get some quick results. Also, to show you that there are at least one hundred cost-effective ways to get solar energy leads and clients.

But this is not a full training book. We have a learn-and-earn program that involves working and shadowing me or other certified solar advisors taking practical steps. Just like we would if were a new real estate agent. We will shadow and work with a seasoned realtor for at least our first few real estate transactions.

Exp Realty, one of the largest cloud-based real estate brokerages https://exprealty.com/ policy is that the new real estate agent shadows and learn from a senior realtor for their first three real estate transactions. The new real estate agent for which shares a small percentage of their commission with the senior realtor within Exp Realty.

Same is in the medical industry in any country since ages that a new student medical doctor who is completing a residency program at the hospital works with a senior medical doctor.

Same with a newly licensed lawyer who works and learns from a senior partner of the law firm. A student who is leaning how to fly an airplane. First co-pilots as a student with the teacher senior pilot. Then, switch places and takes control of the airplane while the senior teacher pilot observes the first flights of the student pilot.

The good news is that in our earn-while-you learn program. One can earn $6000-$9000 within their first 30 days with us. Then, once they observe three sales. They will take a skills test. Pass the interview and then become a certified solar advisor. After becoming a certified solar advisor, when can earn any amount of income they like at their own terms. Sky is the limit!

In human history from day one, every teacher was the student first.

FACTS & LEGAL RESEACH

In 2007, I became a paralegal and worked for top reputable law firms in the United States as a senior paralegal. Part of my job as a paralegal was doing legal research. That was my full-time career for about thirteen years. While I was doing part time energy business from home.

See below my Diploma of Paralegal Studies dated December 19, 2007.

On April 16, 2013, I became admitted before the United States of Court of Appeals for Veterans Claims as a non-attorney practitioner to practice before the said court under a supervision of an attorney.

This is to say that I do have qualified experience, training, and education to do legal search. But not to give legal advice. Only a lawyer can give legal advice and I am not a lawyer so I cannot give legal advice.

But below is my You Tube video that is public information and is legal research that I have done on the topic of solar energy industry. It is not legal advice. It is public information. That is:

What climate change are we expecting in the world?

What climate change are we expecting the U.S.?

The new report from the state of Texas top agency regarding the expected drought in the near future.

Why is FEMA preparing for extreme heat?

What is an Executive Order 14057 from the President Joe Biden?

What did 110 countries agree to do last year in Dubai for the first time ever?

How solar energy can help?

Considering these current and future circumstances, is the solar energy business worth doing?

Please watch my 20 minutes You Tube video titled as

Is Solar Energy Business Worth It? "LEGAL RESEARCH"
www.realtordaddy.com

https://www.youtube.com/watch?v=-uSMH8GG3io&t=130s

My You Tube Channel is "REALTOR DADDY"

I AM A GREEN REALTOR

So, there are over two million plus realtors in the United States according to the National Association of Realtors. Over fifty thousand realtors in Houston, Texas.

Out of which, there are only two thousand realtors in the nation that are Green Realtors. In Houston, only twenty-five realtors are Green Realtors. I am one of them.

So, who is a Green Realtor or a Green Designated Realtor? A Green Realtor is the one that has taken extra education, taken exam, and received credentials from the National Association of Realtors (NAR). A Green realtor is educated to guide the public when it comes to renewable energies and how people can make their home a high-performing efficient and smart home at low cost.

A Green Realtor is familiar with the resources that a homeowner would need when it comes to renewable energy what we call a "Green Curve".

A realtor or a real estate agent without a Green Designation from National Association of Realtor would not be educated as a Green Designated Realtor when it comes to renewable energy and/or solar energy.

In fact, in April 2024, I did a survey. I contacted one hundred different realtors and brokers from various parts of Texas and asked them questions about solar energy systems. All of them had no prior knowledge and experience when it comes to buying or selling real estate that had solar energy systems.

Few of them had nothing good to say. When I asked them, does that have to do with issues you had in transactions with real estate properties with solar panel systems. They answered, yes. But when I asked them how much experience and education they had when it comes to solar panel systems and how to sell or buy homes with solar panels system. They had no knowledge. When I further asked them did you know that you took a listing of a house with a solar panels system knowing that you had no knowledge and experience in dealing with solar panels Green Homes? They became quiet and started learning from me.

Green Homes are a specialty. A realtor must have qualified knowledge in helping to buy or sell Green real estate. So, ask your realtor whether they are a Green Realtor or not before you consider their advice to get involved in doing solar energy business or not.

Here are my credentials. My Texas Real Estate Sales Agent License and my broker's information.

NASIR WAHAB QURESHI
C/O TEXAS SIGNATURE REALTY, LLC
MERT Y ERBIL
2323 S VOSS RD STE 315C
HOUSTON, TX 77057

Real Estate Sales Agent License

Sales Agent: **Nasir Wahab Qureshi**
Sales Agent License #: **792478**   License Expires: **09/30/2024**
Sponsoring Broker: **Texas Signature Realty, LLC**
Sponsoring Broker License #: **9011215**

Having provided satisfactory evidence of the qualifications required by the Texas Real Estate License Act, Occupations Code, Chapter 1101, authorization is granted to use this title: Real Estate Sales Agent

Chelsea Buchholtz
Executive Director

For additional information or to file a complaint please contact TREC at www.trec.texas.gov.

MY GREEN DESIGNATION FROM THE NATIONAL ASSOCIATION OF REALTORS

Nasir Qureshi "Realtor Daddy"

www.realtordaddy.com

Scan for my digital business card or visit www.oneminute.today

ABOUT THE AUTHOR

Nasir Qureshi is a Texas licensed real estate sales agent. Nasir lives with his beautiful wife and three children in Houston, Texas. Nasir has called Houston, Texas his home since 1980.

Nasir has a background being a paralegal at law firms for over 16 years. Nasir further brings his experience of business from the world of direct selling. Nasir speaks 11 different languages and has dedicated himself to personal development since 1997. Nasir is a former newspaper columnist for Houston Inner Looper. He has authored two other books. Both became best-selling books on Amazon. www.nasirqureshi.com

Nasir Qureshi "Realtor Daddy"

TREC Lic # 0792478

Texas Signature Realty

2323 S. Voss Road, Suite 315 C

Houston, Texas 77057

Tel: (281) 857-2000

E-mail: nasir@realtordaddy.com

OTHER BOOKS BY THE AUTHOR ARE AVAILABLE ON AMAZON

(1)

"How Not to Hire A Bad Immigration Lawyer"

(2)

"Bulletproof Mindset for Network Marketing"

(3)

"How to Sell Your House Fast, 53 Tips to Get Full Value, Avoid Seller Pitfall, and Make Your Sale Hassle-Free"

(4)

"Find The Best Realtor In Texas"

MY GIFT FOR YOU

Please enter your e-mail address at www.oneminute.today to get my newsletter. Also, I can do free training for your team and/or your real estate brokerage if you like. It could be online or offline, depending on my schedule and location.

REQUEST FOR YOUR KIND REVIEW

No one is perfect! I am not either. I did my best to provide accurate content in this book. But if you think there is an error in this book. Kindly email me first at nasir@realtordaddy.com for giving me an opportunity to correct it.

If I was able to provide you with at least one helpful idea in this book. Then, I deserve your kind review. It means a lot to me and to my family!

www.ingramcontent.com/pod-product-compliance
Lightning Source LLC
Chambersburg PA
CBHW050247230526
45470CB00005B/2145